D1172730

THE PENGUINS ARE COMING!

by R. L. Penney

Pictures by Tom Eaton

Harper & Row, Publishers • New York, Evanston, and London

THE PENGUINS ARE COMING!

For information address Harper & Row, Publishers, Incorporated, 49 East 33rd Street, New York, N.Y. 10016. Published simultaneously in Canada by Fitzhenry & Whiteside Limited, Toronto.

Trade Standard Book Number 06-024692-8
Harpercrest Standard Book Number 06-024693-6
Library of Congress Catalog Card Number: 78-85027

To my children,

David, Deanna, and Steven

Penguins are birds.
They have feathers and lay eggs.
Their feathers look like fur
because they are small
and close together.
Feathers keep penguins warm and dry
when they swim in the ocean.

There are eighteen kinds of penguins.
I wanted to learn about
Adelie penguins,
so I went to Antarctica.
I got on a big ship
sailing south.

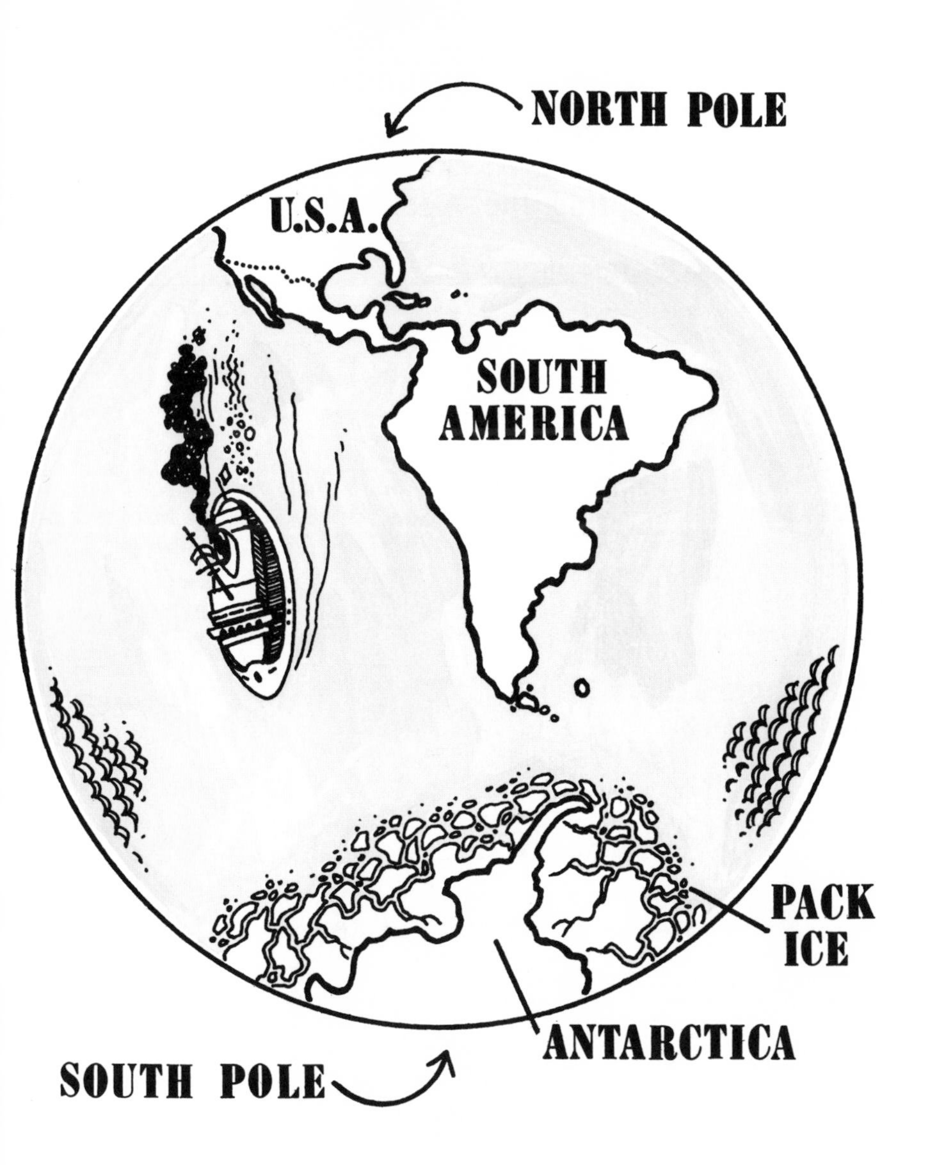
NORTH POLE
U.S.A.
SOUTH AMERICA
PACK ICE
ANTARCTICA
SOUTH POLE

We had to sail through pack ice.
Pack ice is the floating ice
around Antarctica.
Each spring the Adelie penguins
leave the pack ice.

They come to the Antarctic shore
to mate and lay their eggs.
The penguins gather
where there are many stones.
This is where they make their nests.
It is called a rookery.
They use the small stones
to build their nests.

I found a rocky shore
with many piles of stones.
This must be a rookery!
The best way to learn about animals
is to live with them.
I built a house on a sled.
I moved it near the rookery.
Then I waited.

What is that noise?
It sounds like *Aark.*
It must be penguins!
I rush down to the shore.

I look out over the miles of ice.
Little black dots are moving slowly
through the deep snow.
One dot follows another
like a choo-choo train.

Adelie penguins
are only fourteen inches high.
They weigh about fourteen pounds.
This is twice as much
as a new human baby.

The snow is ten inches deep.
The penguins have to work hard
to push through the deep snow.
When the first penguin gets tired,
another penguin takes the lead.

Can I help them through the snow?
I walk toward them.
They stop about twenty feet away
and give their call, *Aark.*
I turn around and drag my feet
to make a path.
The penguins follow me.
Away we go like a train.
Just for fun,
I lead them around in a big circle.
They follow me again.

I go to the shore.
The little train of penguins
comes to the rocky shore too.
They seem friendly to one another.
But when they come
to the piles of stones,
they walk away from one another.

They are not so friendly now.
Each one goes to a different spot.
They point their heads to the sky.
They yell in a loud *Aaaaauaaah.*
Many penguins join in.
Each stands at his special place
in the rookery.

Every day more penguins come
to the big piles of stones.
There are hundreds of penguins.
They all look alike.
I cannot tell which bird is which.
I want to put numbers on each bird.
It is easiest to catch a penguin
when the bird is on its nest.
The nest is its home,
and it does not want to leave.

The best way to pick up a penguin
is to grab it by the neck
and place its head between your knees.
It hits your legs very hard
with its flippers.
I put a metal band on its flipper.
The band has a number on it.

The band does not hurt the bird.
The numbers help me
to tell the birds apart.
I put stakes by their piles of stones.
The stakes have numbers too.
Now I can tell where they live.

When I let a penguin go,
it runs back to its nest.
Then I sit down to watch the penguins.
I use a telescope to read the numbers.
I write down everything
the penguins do.

The first Adelie penguins to come
to a rookery are male penguins.
A male penguin seems to care most
about its nest.
He needs a nest for himself,
his mate, and their little penguins.
If someone tries to take it away,
he will fight very hard.
He will almost always win.

The female penguins arrive
a few days later.
When a male and female meet at the nest,
they make a loud noise.
It sounds like a stick rattling
on a picket fence.
The male and female
wave their heads together.
Then they begin to collect stones
to build their nest.

Explorers used to think
that male penguins gave stones
to the females as presents.
This is not true.
The male and female take turns
collecting stones.

One of them always stays on the nest.
Other penguins will steal the stones
if the nest is not guarded.
Penguins fight with a tough peck.
They beat each other
with their flippers.

For two weeks
the penguins build their nests.
It is springtime in Antarctica.
The sun shines both day and night.
The birds do not eat or sleep.
The male and female penguins
take turns guarding their nests.
They stand close to each other.

One day the female lays an egg.
The penguins scream
Aaaaaaugh, aaaaaugh, aaaugh.
They wave their heads.

Two or three days later,
the female lays another egg.
Again they yell
Aaaaugh, aaaaugh, aaugh.

Now the male penguin gets on the nest
to keep the eggs warm.
A penguin has a place on its body
with no feathers.
It is called an incubation patch.
This patch is warm.
It keeps the eggs warm.
The female is hungry
after she lays her two eggs.
She has not eaten for two weeks.
Her only food is in the sea.
She collects a few more stones,
and the male places them on the nest.

Then away she goes to an ice cliff.
Many female penguins stand at the edge.
They push and shove.

Suddenly one jumps into the water.

The others jump too.

There is danger below the cliff.

Leopard Seals wait in the sea.

They eat penguins when they jump in.

Most of the penguins get away.

They swim north.

They eat small shrimp in the sea.

Soon they will be fat again.

Back at the nest,
the eggs must be kept warm.
The male penguin sits on the nest.
Sometimes the winds blow
more than one hundred miles an hour.
Still the male sits—
even when he is almost covered with snow.

Two weeks go by.
The eggs are warm.
No one has stolen the nest stones.
The male penguin is skinny.
He has not eaten for over a month.
He has been living on his body fat.

At last the females come back.
I see them popping in and out of the water.
They jump up.
They swim under the water.
Then they jump up again for air.
Finally they pop up onto the ice cliff.
They call out *Aark*.

The penguins put oil on their feathers.
This keeps the feathers waterproof and shiny.
The oil comes from a special place
above the tail.
They rub the gland with their bills.
Then they rub their bills
on their feathers.
This is called preening.

When a female gets near her nest,
she suddenly runs and calls loudly.
Her mate answers
in shattering calls.
The noise of all the penguins
is so loud
it can be heard a mile away.

They wave their heads.
They bow to the nest and the eggs.
The male penguin slowly lifts his feet
and moves off the nest.
He seems tired and stiff.
The female quickly covers the eggs.
Now the male can go to sea and feed.
He gathers more nest stones,
then he waves his head to his mate.
The males gather at the beach.
They too must jump
past the Leopard Seals.
The penguins need a bath
and many pounds of shrimp.

For thirty-five days
the penguins keep the eggs warm.
Then the eggs hatch.
Something peeps in each nest.
Something breaks a small hole in the egg
and pops out.
When penguin chicks hatch,
they look like gray fuzzy balls.
You could hold one
in your hands.
Peep, peep.
The chicks want food.

The father penguin comes back
from the sea.
His stomach is full of food.
The chick peeps
and reaches up for food.
He sticks his small bill
into his father's bill.
The male penguin forces food
up from his stomach.
The chick gobbles it down.
Then the chick sleeps.
Another chick bursts out of its egg.
It is also hungry.

Now the female goes to sea again.
She comes back.
Her stomach is full of food.
She covers the chicks
to keep them warm.
When they peep or beg for food,
she feeds them.

When the chicks are three weeks old,
both parents rush to the sea
for more food.
The young are alone.
There are no big penguins
to keep them safe.

The South Polar skua
is also hungry.
The skua is a big bird.
His wingspread is
about five feet.
He eats fish, sea animals,
penguin eggs, and penguin chicks.
The skua is not a bad bird.
He is just hungry.
He has his own chicks to feed.

The penguin chicks gather in clubs
called “creches.”
The chicks are safe when they are together.
And the chicks keep warm
in the big bundle.
When a parent penguin comes back
and gives a call,
two of the gray fuzzy balls jump up.

They run back to their own nest.
There they are fed.
Sometimes other chicks come too.
But the big penguin only feeds its own chicks.
I know this
because I put bands on the chicks
after they hatched.
I know which chicks belong to which parents.

When they are five weeks old,
the chicks are very fat.
Their stomachs drag on the ground.
They can eat as much as they weigh.

When the chicks
are seven or eight weeks old,
the adults go away
to feed in the sea.
They do not come back.
The chicks are all alone.
Winter is coming.
It starts to get colder
and very windy.
What will the chicks do now?
Their only food is in the sea.

The chicks go down to the beaches.
As they run,
their little fuzzy feathers fall off.
The chicks were once gray.
Now they are black and white
like big penguins.
Like their parents,
they oil their feathers.

They oil and oil.

They whirr and whirr their flippers.

They are ready to go to sea.

The ocean waves are big and frightening.

The chicks begin to call a weak *Aark*.

This is the call to go.

A big piece of ice
comes floating along the shore.
The chicks suddenly jump into the water
and swim for the ice.
Crash! Crash!
The waves bury them.
Some turn back.
A few chicks scramble up on the ice
and slowly float away to sea.
Soon other chicks follow.

They will stay in the pack ice
for a few years.
Then they return to the rookery.
They will be old enough
to raise baby penguins themselves.

I wait seven months
for another spring
and the return of the penguins.
I want to know
if the hundreds of banded penguins
will come back to the same rookery.
Will they keep their same nests
and the same mates and neighbors?

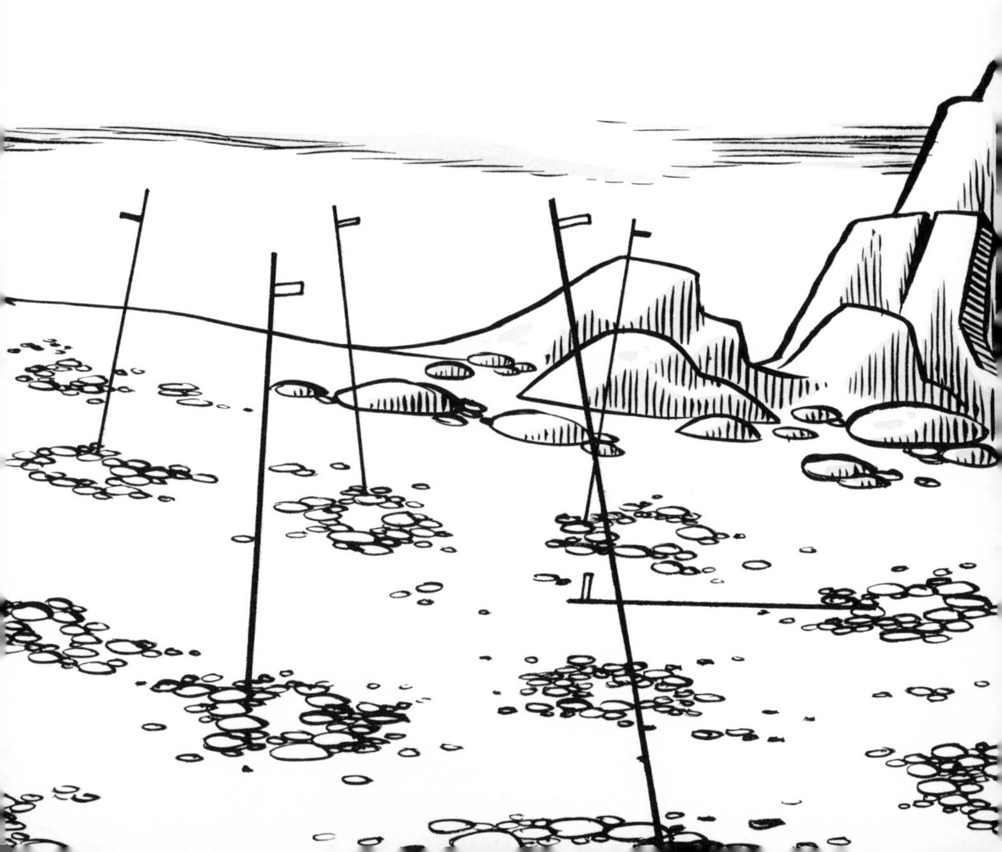

Here comes a group!
Through the telescope
I can see that some are banded.
Again the male penguins
are the first to come.

I hide behind rocks and snowdrifts
and watch banded penguins
to see where they go.
Amazing!
The males return to the very same places
they built nests the year before.
I check them with my maps and notebooks.

The males get excited
when they reach
their old nesting places.
They fight other males
standing near their territory.
They are noisy too!
They seem happy to be back.
In a few days the females
land on the icy shore.
They rush up
to their old nesting places
and greet their mates.
They yell loud *Aaaughs*.
And then, one by one,
the male and female penguins
begin to rebuild their nests.

About Dr. R. L. Penney

Dr. Penney has made five trips to Antarctica to study Adelie penguins. He has spent forty-one months there.

He also studies Adelie penguins in a laboratory at the New York Zoological Society in the Bronx Zoo. He wants to learn what their motions and sounds mean and how they find their way from one place to another.

He is planning another trip to Antarctica. This time he hopes to study the Adelie penguins in the water from a submarine.